Well-Behaved Children

100 Tips From Parents Who Have Them

DEVRA DOIRON

SEAVIEW PRESS
Lahaina, Hawaii

Published by SEAVIEW PRESS
5095 Napilihau St. Pmb. 121
Lahaina, HI 96761

Publisher's Cataloging-in-Publication Data
Doiron, Devra
    Well-behaved children: 100 tips from parents who have
    them / Devra Doiron – Lahaina, Hawaii: Seaview Press,
    2000.
        p.   cm.

    ISBN 0-9678615-0-0
    1. Discipline of children. 2. Parenting.   I. Title.
HQ770 .4 D65   2000   99-91936
649/.64   dc—21   CIP

PROJECT COORDINATION BY JENKINS GROUP, INC.

03 02 01 00 ❖ 5 4 3 2 1

Printed in the United States of America

To the Ledbetters, the Tuckers, the Tullochs,
and the Wainios, without whom this book,
and my own well-behaved children,
would not have been possible.

Contents

One: Basic Concepts

1. *Start Immediately* 2. *Understand the Law of Reinforcement* 3. *Reinforce Good Behavior* 4. *Make Clear Rules* 5. *Be Consistent* 6. *Don't Lose Control* 7. *Never Make Idle Threats* 8. *Be Firm, Not Dominating* 9. *One Warning, Then the Judgement* 10. *Each Child is Different* 11. *Change When Necessary* 12. *Discipline Equals Love* 13. *Never Discipline in Anger* 14. *Time-out* 15. *Length of a Time-out* 16. *Three Strikes, You're Out* 17. *Creative Discipline* 18. *Incentives* 19. *Reward Quickly* 20. *Choose Your Battles Carefully* 21. *Build Self-Esteem* 22. *Teach Them Self-Control* 23. *The Punishment Should Fit the Crime*

Two: Family Relations

24. *Earn Your Child's Respect* 25. *Don't Be Manipulated* 26. *Communicate Respectfully* 27. *Admit When You're Wrong* 28. *Both Parents in Agreement* 29. *No Name Calling* 30. *Examine Your Priorities* 31. *Family Meetings* 32. *Everyone Helps*

Contents

33. *Keeping the Faith* 34. *Encourage Hugs* 35. *Love Your Child Unconditionally* 36. *Insist on Good Manners*

Three: Young Children

37. *Teach the Meaning of "No"* 38. *Discipline for Toddlers* 39. *Set Boundaries for Young Children*
40. *Sharing* 41. *No Counting* 42. *No Yelling*
43. *Temper Tantrums* 44. *Tantrums in Public*
45. *Whining* 46. *Hitting* 47. *Tattling* 48. *Biting*
49. *Excessive Crying* 50. *Fighting Over Toys*
51. *Coming When Called* 52. *Discipline While on the Phone* 53. *Restaurant Behavior* 54. *Boredom*
55. *Excess Energy* 56. *Don't Try to Reason with a Toddler* 57. *Give Choices* 58. *Quiet Time* 59. *Pay Attention* 60. *Bedtime Woes* 61. *What Time is Bedtime?* 62. *Lights Out* 63. *Bedtime is Not a Social Hour* 64. *Caring for Younger Siblings* 65. *Taking Care of Themselves* 66. *Five-Minute Warning*
67. *Immaturity or Willful Disobedience?*
68. *Traveling* 69. *Picky Eaters* 70. *Save it for Later*
71. *Nutritious Foods First* 72. *Cleaning the Plate*
73. *Limit the Sugar* 74. *Food Allergies*
75. *Disruptive Behavior in a Group* 76. *Discipline in Public* 77. *Keep Them Fed and Rested*

Four: Older Children

78. *Sibling Rivalry*   79. *Balance & Moderation*
80. *Being Considerate of Others*   81. *The Oldest Child*
82. *Discipline Privately*   83. *Don't Nag*   84. *Suffering the Consequences*   85. *Allowances Should Be Earned*
86. *Taking a Stand*   87. *Laziness*   88. *Discuss Improvement*   89. *Constant Requests*   90. *Television Influence*   91. *Internet Influence*   92. *Put Them to Work*   93. *Fashion Battles*   94. *Bad Attitudes*
95. *Don't Overindulge Them*   96. *Mutual Benefits*
97. *Express Gratitude*   98. *Cleaning Their Rooms*
99. *No Arguments* 100. *Don't Expect Perfection*

Introduction

When my husband and I were first married, we contemplated not having children. We knew that children were supposed to be a great source of joy, but after years of observing families in restaurants, parks and malls, we believed that all children behaved poorly and caused their parents a great deal of stress and aggravation. Eventually, however, we met some families who were different. Their children were a pleasure to be around, and we soon discovered why. The parents of the well-behaved children all had one thing in common: they practiced effective, consistent discipline. These parents had developed specific rules for acceptable behavior, and those rules were strictly enforced. This resulted in healthy, well-adjusted children, as well as relaxed, happy parents. We observed these families closely, and we learned from them.

Now, many years later, my husband and I are the proud parents of three wonderfully well-behaved kids of our own. We are thrilled every time someone comes up to us in a restaurant or on an airplane and compliments us on the children's behavior. We are frequently asked by other parents what our "secret" is. Our secret, of course, is to gather tips from parents of other remarkably well-behaved children, and to apply those tips.

This book contains the collective wisdom of those happy families.

BASIC
CONCEPTS

1. Start Immediately

It's never too early or too late to train a child to be compliant and well-mannered. The older the child is, the more effort it will take, but it can be done. Instead of finding excuses for your child's misbehavior, take action. Train yourself to be diligent and consistent, then experiment with different methods of reward and punishment until you find what works best for your family.

"Let the child's first lesson be obedience, and the second will be what thou wilt." - Benjamin Franklin

2. Understand the Law of Reinforcement

The Law of Reinforcement states: Behavior which achieves desirable consequences will continue to occur; behavior which achieves undesirable consequences will cease. This is the most important thing to understand when trying to raise well-behaved children. For example, if a child throws a temper tantrum and gets what he wants, he will continue to throw tantrums. If that behavior results in punishment instead, he will no longer use this method.

"Many parents are so influenced by psychological theories about child rearing that they disregard common sense." - P. Dalton

3. Reinforce Good Behavior

The Law of Reinforcement also applies to good behavior. When good behavior achieves a desirable effect, children are more likely to repeat it. Parents tend to reprimand their children frequently throughout the day, but fail to acknowledge the times when the children are behaving well. Let your child know that you've noticed his good behavior and that you appreciate it.

"Immediate reinforcement is the most useful technique available to parents in teaching responsibility to their children." - Dr. James Dobson

4. Make Clear Rules

Never punish a child for something she didn't know was wrong. When a child misbehaves in a way that was never previously discussed, take her aside and explain that the behavior is unacceptable. Decide right then what the punishment will be for breaking this rule in the future, and be sure the child understands. Don't leave any question in her mind as to how you'll react. If a child knows a crime carries a stiff penalty, she probably won't commit it.

"Call them rules or call them limits...they are an expression of loving concern." - Mister Rogers

5. Be Consistent

In order to be effective, a rule must be enforced every time it's broken. When you are tired or distracted, it's tempting to overlook misbehavior. Don't be tempted. Children will continue to break rules if they feel there is a chance they'll get away with it. Inconsistency is the number one reason most discipline techniques fail.

"Children are unpredictable. You never know what inconsistency they're going to catch you in next."
- Franklin P. Jones

6. Don't Lose Control

Sometimes kids enjoy causing their parents to shout, cry, or otherwise lose control. If you allow your children to have that kind of power over you, they will see it as a sign of weakness, and they will exploit it. (Remember how much fun it was to torment an inexperienced substitute teacher?) No matter how stressful the situation, maintain control of your voice and actions. Take a deep breath and count to ten. If you still feel the need to go ballistic, do it out of range of the kids.

"You know you've lost control when you're the one who goes to your room." - Babs Bell Hajdusiewicz

7. Never Make Idle Threats

If you make a threat and don't follow through, you'll weaken your credibility and lose respect. If you tell your child you'll throw away his shoes if he leaves them on the stairs again, he knows you won't do that because you'll then have to buy him new shoes. If you tell your teen you'll take away her car for a whole month, she'll know you won't follow through because you'll have to drive her to school every day. Think carefully before making a threat, and don't say it if you don't mean it.

"Explain the concept of death very carefully to your child. This will make threatening him with it much more effective." - P. J. O'Rourke

8. Be Firm, Not Dominating

I t's important to have strict rules governing behavior, but don't be too dominating. A child whose every action is rigidly controlled could end up with debilitating dependency or hostility. Be sure to allow your child the opportunity to make some decisions on her own, and allow her considerable freedom on issues of minor importance.

> *"The most assiduous task of parenting is to divine the difference between boundaries and bondage."*
> *- Barbara Kingsolver*

9. One Warning, Then the Judgement

Some ineffective parents give multiple warnings before following through with punishment. This sends a message to the child that he does not have to cease the undesirable behavior immediately. He knows that his behavior will be tolerated for a while, and he continues to misbehave until the parent finally decides to enforce. It's more effective to give the child just one warning, and if the misbehavior occurs again, then discipline quickly follows.

"There are two great injustices that can befall a child. One is to punish him for something he didn't do. The other is to let him get away with something he knows is wrong." - Robert Gardner

10. Each Child is Different

As any parent of more than one child knows, children are born with distinct personalities, and no two are exactly alike. Even if you raise two children identically, they will not be identical in behavior or temperament. Time-outs may be very effective for an active child, but have no effect on her calm sister. You may need to use different discipline methods for each child.

"Nature made him and then broke the mold."
- Ludovico Ariosto

11. Change When Necessary

If what you're doing isn't working, try something else. It's a logical concept, but many parents don't practice this. They give their small children increasingly longer time-outs, or ground their teenager for a longer period of time, but the children continue to misbehave. Children change as they grow, and the discipline method that worked last week may not work this week. Keep trying other methods until you find one that works well for you now.

"A capacity to change is indispensable."
- John Foster Dulles

12. Discipline Equals Love

Make sure your children know that you discipline them because you love them. Tell them this after punishment has been administered. When the crying and anger have ceased, hug your child and tell him that you are sorry you had to punish him, but you did so because you love him and want to be sure he grows up to be a healthy, responsible adult.

"He who spares the rod hates his son, but he who loves him is careful to discipline him." - Proverbs 3:24

13. Never Discipline in Anger

Never administer discipline when feeling angry or out of control. Go to another room for a few moments until you feel calm, then administer the punishment. It helps to have a previously agreed upon consequence for breaking a rule, because in the heat of battle, you may not be able to think clearly, and you may later regret your actions.

"Children need love, especially when they do not deserve it." - Harold Hulbert

14. Time-out

Time-out is the most common form of discipline for small children, but it's only effective when used properly. When your child misbehaves or gets too rowdy, send him to an out-of-the way location for a specified amount of time. Toddlers can be placed in an empty playpen or in a room with a baby gate. Other children should be sent to a corner, where they must face the wall and sit quietly until the time-out is over. It's important that you don't allow the child to talk, watch TV, or play with toys during time-out.

> *"When my kids become wild and unruly, I use a nice, safe playpen. When they're finished, I climb out."*
> *- Erma Bombeck*

15. Length of a Time-out

A good way to determine the length of a time-out, is to use the child's age. A two-year-old should stay for two minutes. A three-year-old for three minutes, etc. If the child refuses to sit quietly until the time is up, you'll have to resort to a stronger form of discipline, perhaps a long stay in her room or revoke a privilege like dessert or TV.

"You can learn many things from children. How much patience you have, for instance."
- Franklin P. Jones

16. Three Strikes, You're Out

Many children respond well to the "Three Strike Method." If a child misbehaves, tell him it's "strike one." If he misbehaves again, "strike two." After three strikes, take a privilege away for the rest of the day. Good privileges to revoke include watching TV, playing with friends, Nintendo time, etc. If the child continues to misbehave, continue to revoke privileges.

"Before I got married, I had six theories about bringing up children. Now I have six children and no theories." - John Wilmot

17. Creative Discipline

Be creative when deciding which discipline method is best for your child. Take into account his likes and dislikes. If skateboarding is his favorite pastime, revoke that privilege for a few days. A socialite teen can be grounded, a chore hater given extra chores, etc. If you run out of ideas, consult with friends and family about which methods worked for their child, and give those a try. Eventually you'll discover what motivates your child to behave.

"Foolishness is bound in the heart of a child, but the rod of discipline will drive it far from him."
- Proverbs 22:15

18. Incentives

It's always better to reward good behavior than to punish bad behavior. Decide what is important to your child, and use it as an incentive. You might try offering a trip to the video arcade on Saturday in exchange for not fighting with siblings all week. Or maybe a special dessert could be used as a reward for maintaining a good attitude. Be creative, and choose rewards which appeal to your child.

"A father is someone who carries pictures where his money used to be." - Anonymous

19. Reward Quickly

When using a reward for good behavior, be sure it's something that can be granted quickly, or it will lose its value. For example, don't promise your child a trip to Disneyland next summer if she can be good until then. Next summer may be so far away, it will not keep your child motivated for long. Instead, use smaller rewards as incentives so that they can be given out sooner.

"Why take your kids to Disneyland when for the same money you can put them through college?"
- Bruce Lansky

20. Choose Your Battles Carefully

No child is perfect, and your children will no doubt do many things throughout the day of which you don't approve. If you harass them about every little thing, they will just tune you out. Instead, concentrate your efforts on the important things, and try to overlook the minor ones. Forgetting to make the bed is not worth getting upset over, but breaking curfew is.

> *"There will be plenty of real issues that require you to stand like a rock. Save your big guns for those crucial confrontations." - Dr. James C. Dobson*

21. Build Self-Esteem

Poor self-esteem is the root cause of many emotional and behavioral problems for children, teenagers, and even adults. By building up your child's self-image during his early years, you will be giving him a lifelong gift. Hug your child and tell him how much he's loved at least once a day. Compliment him frequently, even on little things. Choose your words carefully when disciplining him, being careful not to attack his character, only his actions. For example, don't say, "Why can't you do anything right?" Instead say, "Please do it again, and do it correctly this time."

"Self-esteem isn't everything; it's just that there's nothing without it." - Gloria Steinem

22. Teach them Self-Control

Kids should be allowed to have fun, but discourage behavior which is wild and out of control. When in public, insist that your children stay right next to you. When near breakable items in a store, have them keep their hands on their elbows, and teach them to look with their eyes, not with their hands. Whether at home or away, self-control significantly reduces the need for discipline.

"If you can win complete mastery over self, you will easily master all else." - Thomas Kempis

23. The Punishment Should Fit the Crime

I f each transgression is treated equally, children will never learn which issues are important. For example, a young child might receive a time-out for running in the house, but a long stay in his room for fighting with his sister. For older children, if forgetting to do a chore results in the same punishment as telling a lie, the child will not learn how bad it is to lie. A stiffer penalty will help him to understand this vitally important issue.

"The punishment shall fit the offense." - Cicero

FAMILY
RELATIONS

24. Earn Your Child's Respect

Respect is not given. It's earned. Your child will not treat you with dignity if you will not do the same for him. Let him know that you value his feelings and opinions, and never ridicule him. And remember, it's much better to have your children obey you out of respect than out of fear.

"Developing respect for the parents is the critical factor in child management." - Dr. James Dobson

25. Don't be Manipulated

Earn the right to control your child by proving to him you are capable of the job. If you allow your child to manipulate you in any way, you will lose credibility. Little girls know they can soften daddy's heart with tears, and teenagers instinctively know how to use your guilt to their advantage. Be aware of the ways children manipulate their parents, and be on your guard.

> "The thing that impresses me most about America is the way parents obey their children."
> - Duke of Windsor

26. Communicate Respectfully

A child should be encouraged to say anything that's on her mind, as long as it's said in a respectful manner. If your child feels you've dealt unfairly with her, she should be allowed to express her feelings, but she must not be disrespectful in any way. By encouraging open communication, you can show her you respect her opinions, even if you disagree with them.

"Few parents nowadays pay any regard to what their children say to them. The old-fashioned respect for the young is fast dying out." - Oscar Wilde

27. Admit When You're Wrong

Parents occasionally make mistakes and pass judgement too quickly before having all the facts. It's important to apologize for a mistake as soon as you discover you've made it. Some parents think that by admitting a mistake to a child, they will lose power and credibility. The opposite is true. When parents admit to a mistake and apologize for it, they model good character, and gain their children's respect and trust.

"Happy will that house be in which the relations are formed from character." - Ralph Waldo Emerson

28. Both Parents in Agreement

Both parents should agree on rules and methods of discipline so that when one or the other is alone with the child, the discipline is the same. When parents have different rules, children get confused. Worse yet, the children will learn to "play" one parent against the other. ("Dad lets us do it!")

"Having a child is surely the most beautifully irrational act that two people in love can commit."
- Bill Cosby

29. No Name Calling

Never allow children to be disrespectful to you or to anyone else. Teach your kids that it's okay to be angry with someone, but they must express that anger without name calling. Outlaw the use of words such as "stupid," "hate," and "idiot." Instead, encourage your children to express themselves without resorting to meanness and harsh words.

"The tongue is not steel, yet it cuts." - *George Herbert*

30. Examine Your Priorities

If you make your children a priority in your life, they will be more likely to want to please you with good behavior. If your child is involved in sports, go to the games. If you think missing a few won't matter to the child, you're deceiving yourself. Many adults today still harbor resentment and hurt feelings because their parents didn't make time for them and take an interest in their activities.

> *"Children begin by loving their parents. After a time they judge them. Rarely, if ever, do they forgive them."*
> *- Oscar Wilde*

31. Family Meetings

As children grow, have them participate in family meetings to discuss attitudes and ways to improve less-than-perfect behavior. This is a good way to show them that you value and respect their opinions and suggestions.

"Discipline is not a silent affair. It requires that you and your child talk and relate to each other."
- Dr. William P. Garvey

32. Everyone Helps

Insist that your children help with household duties. Even a young child can set the table and put things away. Older children should take out the trash, do dishes and help with the laundry. By insisting that your children complete chores each day, you will be teaching them responsibility, teamwork and how to follow instructions.

> *"Where parents do too much for their children, children will not do much for themselves."*
> *- Elbert Hubbard*

33. Keeping the Faith

If you want your children to share in your religious faith and behave appropriately, then model this behavior for them. Start teaching them about God at an early age. Read Bible stories to them and play children's worship tapes in your home. When they behave poorly, encourage them to ask God for forgiveness. Talk frequently about God's love for them, and how they are always to be respectful of Him.

"Train up a child in the way he should go, and when he is old, he will not depart from it." (Proverbs 22:6)

34. Encourage Hugs

Siblings compete with each other constantly for attention and toys, and that makes life stressful for everyone in the home. Insist that your children apologize to each other after an altercation, and encourage hugging. One of the nicest things you can do for your children is to promote bonding between them.

"For there is no friend like a sister, in calm or stormy weather." - Christina Rossetti

35. Love Your Child Unconditionally

Tell your children that no matter what, you will always love them. Many behavior problems are the result of a child feeling unloved, and the child retaliates against his parents with bad behavior. Demonstrate your love by hugging your kids every day, even the older ones. Older children, especially boys, may pretend to dislike your affection, but don't believe it. Everyone needs the human touch, even if it's just a pat on the back or a squeeze of the shoulder.

> *"The greatest gifts my parents gave to me...were their unconditional love and a set of values."*
> *- Colin Powell*

36. Insist on Good Manners

If you want your children to exhibit good manners, saying "Please," "Thank you," and "Excuse me," should be mandatory, even at home. Many parents expect their children to be polite in public, but it's not expected in the home. Unfortunately, good manners are difficult for children unless they are practiced every day.

"Children are natural mimics; they act like their parents in spite of our efforts to teach them good manners." - Anonymous

YOUNG
CHILDREN

37. Teach the Meaning of "No"

It's important to start a pattern of good discipline as soon as a baby begins to crawl. When the child reaches for something that's off limits: the first time, tell her "NO." The second time, repeat the command, and remove her from the area.

"Those that do teach young babes do it with gentle means and easy tasks." - William Shakespeare

38. Discipline for Toddlers

Unlike babies, toddlers are capable of understanding rules and warnings. If your toddler breaks a rule, tell him, "NO," and tell him he will be given a time-out if it happens again. If it does happen again, immediately put him in time-out. Afterwards, give him a hug, tell him you love him, and remind him of why he was disciplined.

"Toddlers are more likely to eat healthy food if they find it on the floor." - Jan Blaustone

39. Set Boundaries for Young Children

A good way to teach crawling babies and toddlers about the boundaries of acceptable behavior is to allow them access to one cupboard only. Fill this cupboard with things they love to play with, such as wooden spoons, plastic containers, etc. Because young children love to open cupboards and play with the contents, this is a good way to teach limits. ("You may play in this cupboard, but not the others.")

"I don't know why they say 'you have a baby.' The baby has you." - Gallagher

40. Sharing

The concept of sharing is difficult for young children to understand. It takes time for a child to learn to put others before himself. Encourage sharing, but never force a child to give up his toys and snacks to another. Doing so would only cause resentment and exacerbate the problem. Instead, make sure each child is given his own portion of toys and snacks, and praise him when he chooses to share.

> *"He who has two coats, let him share with him who has none. And he who has food, let him do likewise."*
> *- John the Baptist*

41. No Counting

It's common for a parent to count to three aloud before taking action against misbehavior. Her children know that they can continue to ignore their mother while she slowly counts. Only when she reaches the number "three" do they need to stop the undesirable behavior. Not only is this method ineffective, it can also be dangerous. Consider the toddler who reaches up for a pot of boiling water on the stove. The mother sees this from across the room and yells for the child to stop. The child who is accustomed to hearing her mother count to three may continue to reach for the pot because she knows she doesn't have to obey until she hears the word "three." It would be much better for her if she had been trained to obey immediately.

> *"Normally, children learn to gauge rather accurately from the tone of their parent's voice how seriously to take his threats. Of course, they sometimes misjudge and pay the penalty." - Louis Kaplan*

42. No Yelling

Parents who yell create children who yell. If you prefer peace and quiet in your home, teach your children to be quiet. Keep your own voice down, even when angry. Gently remind the children every time they're being loud, and send them outdoors or to separate rooms if necessary. A peaceful, quiet home is easy to achieve if you diligently pursue it.

> *"A child enters your home and for the next twenty years makes so much noise you can hardly stand it. The child departs, leaving the house so silent you think you are going mad." - John Andrew Holmes*

43. Temper Tantrums

The best way to handle a temper tantrum is to ignore it. If you try to reason with a child who is in the middle of a full-blown tantrum; you'll just make matters worse. Never give in to a child's demands during or after a tantrum. If you do, then the child will use this method again and again. Children throw tantrums to get what they want because they think it might work. If you prove to them that it never, ever works and results in punishment, then the tantrums will cease. One caution, though, some children endanger themselves during tantrums by banging their head against the wall or floor, and they need to be restrained. If this occurs, hug the child tightly until he exhausts himself, but do not give in to his demands!

"No appeasement will avoid necessary battles. It only makes them more costly and lengthy."
- Gustave Le Bon

44. Tantrums in Public

Unfortunately, some temper tantrums occur in public. Ignoring tantrums at home is easy, but it's very hard to do in the middle of a crowded grocery store. When this happens, you have two choices, both of which work quite well. You can either ignore the tantrum and the annoyed onlookers while you continue your shopping, or you can leave your grocery cart right there in the aisle, carry your child out to the car, buckle her into her car seat, roll down the windows for air, then wait patiently next to the car for a few minutes until she's finished. Afterward, take the child back into the grocery store and resume your shopping. And of course, do not buy the child whatever she was screaming for in the first place, or you can expect a repeat performance during next week's shopping trip.

"I was doing the family grocery shopping accompanied by two children, an event I hope to see included in the Olympics in the near future."
- Anna Quindlen

45. Whining

Why do some children whine instead of speaking in a normal voice? The answer is simple: because it works. Parents and other care givers can't stand the whining, so they give the child what she wants. This, of course, reinforces the behavior. The child soon learns that whining results in a quick reward, so she continues to do it. To stop the whining habit, don't ever respond favorably to it. Refuse to give the child what she wants until she asks you in a "good" voice, and insist that all other care givers do the same.

"Would you like some cheese to go with that whine?"
- Anonymous

46. Hitting

Some children resort to physical violence as a way of dealing with frustration. This must be discouraged immediately, or it will become a habit which is hard to break. Every time your child hits someone, tell him hitting is unacceptable, and put him into time-out. (Place a toddler into a playpen or behind a baby gate.) After the time-out, suggest a better way of handling disputes, and tell him he will not be allowed to play with others if the problem continues.

"If scientists can put a man on the moon, why can't they figure out which kid hit the other first?"
- Bruce Lansky

47. Tattling

Constant tattling can be one of the most annoying things a parent encounters. Children who tattle excessively do so because they receive positive reinforcement for it. They enjoy having the power to make Mom stop what she's doing and deal with the situation. If you want to stop unnecessary tattling, you must stop giving that positive reinforcement. Make it clear to the tattler that unless something really bad or dangerous is happening, you don't want to hear about it. (Don't worry, even a young child knows what constitutes "really bad" and "dangerous.") If the child continues to tattle unnecessarily, tell her that both she and her sibling will be punished, the sibling for committing the offense, and the other for tattling. If you follow through on this threat every time, your tattling woes are over.

"Parents are not interested in justice, they are interested in quiet." - Bill Cosby

48. Biting

Children bite for different reasons. Some do it out of meanness, and others are merely teething. Regardless of the reason, it must be stopped immediately because a small child's teeth are capable of inflicting tissue damage and even infection. When a child bites, immediately and emphatically tell him, "NO BITING!" and tap him very gently on the lips. Do not strike him hard! The intention is not to inflict pain, but to mildly startle him and draw attention to the offending object. For most children, this is enough. After a few more bites with the same results, they stop biting. Some children, however, need to be punished with a time-out after each incident. If the child is old enough to understand, explain why he is being punished, and that he will not be allowed to play with others because he bites.

"There are times when parenthood seems nothing but feeding the mouth that bites you." - Peter De Vries

49. Excessive Crying

If a child cries because she's hurt, of course you should respond lovingly. However, if a child is crying out of habit or to get attention, it should be discouraged. Tell her she may cry if she wants to, but she must go to another room and shut the door so as not to disturb others. Without an audience, unwarranted crying will soon come to an end.

> *"To this hour I cannot really understand why little children are not just as constantly laughing as they are constantly crying." - Georg Christoph Lichtenberg*

50. Fighting Over Toys

If your children fight over a toy, the most effective way of dealing with the situation is to take the toy away from both of them for a short period of time. This way, you eliminate the argument of "who had it first." It might seem unfair to punish the child who really did have it first, but knowing the consequences will encourage them both to settle their disputes amicably. If the situation keeps repeating itself, however, secretly watch them to see if one child is always the source of trouble, then act appropriately. This way, you can avoid punishing the innocent one.

> *"Nothing brings out a toddler's devotion to a toy she has abandoned more quickly than another child playing with it." - Robert Scotellaro*

51. Coming When Called

Many children refuse to come when called. They're having a good time playing and don't want to stop, so they pretend they can't hear the parent calling them. This problem is easily solved. If your child refuses to come inside when called, and you know he heard you, go get him immediately. Tell him that as punishment for his disobedience, he will not be allowed to play outside tomorrow. Follow through with the punishment, and you probably won't be ignored again. This method also works well for children refusing to get out of the swimming pool, refusing to get off the phone, etc.

"Always end the name of your child with a vowel, so that when you yell, the name will carry." - Bill Cosby

52. Discipline While on the Phone

Many children misbehave intentionally when their mother is on the phone. That's because the children have learned that when Mom is on the phone or otherwise distracted, she does not discipline them. This offers the children a rare opportunity to break the rules without fear of punishment. The solution to this is simple: ask the caller to excuse you for a moment, set the phone down, and administer the usual discipline. The children will soon realize that they can't get away with misbehavior even when you're on the phone, and they will stop trying.

"If evolution really works, how come mothers only have two hands?" - Milton Berle

53. Restaurant Behavior

A child who misbehaves in a restaurant can be very annoying to people seated at nearby tables. It's important to teach children at an early age how to behave appropriately in a restaurant: no yelling, no crying, no throwing things, and definitely no running around the room. With the exception of using the restroom, the child should stay seated until it's time to leave. When a young child misbehaves during a meal, take him to the car for a time-out or your usual disciplinary method. Afterward, take the child back into the restaurant and resume your meal. You might need to repeat this a few times, but the child will soon learn that misbehavior will not be tolerated in a restaurant.

"Raising kids is part joy and part guerilla warfare."
- Ed Asner

54. Boredom

Don't expect good behavior from a bored child. If she'll be spending time in a waiting room or at a relative's house, bring along toys like handheld video games, coloring books, and other quiet distractions.

"When children are doing nothing, they are doing mischief." - Henry Fielding

55. Excess Energy

If children can't expend energy in a positive way, they'll do it in a negative way, usually by misbehavior, whining, or bickering with siblings. When traveling, take time each day to let kids run around in a park and burn off energy. For rainy days at home, invent physical activity games which can be played inside. Also, consider buying a tiny exercise trampoline. It makes a great indoor toy for kids, and alleviates their desire to jump on the bed.

"The dough we spent on Disney World we could have saved instead; the ride the kids remember most was jumping on the bed." - Charles Ghigna

56. Don't Try to Reason With a Toddler

Many parents are reluctant to take advantage of their superior strength when it comes to controlling a defiant child. They have a misguided notion that using force will somehow harm the child psychologically. Sometimes, though, it's the best way to solve a problem. For example, if your toddler refuses to climb into her car seat, don't try to reason with her. Just pick her up and fasten her into the seat. If a temper tantrum ensues, just stand outside the car until she has exhausted herself. She will soon learn that resistance is futile.

"Reasoning with a two-year-old is about as productive as changing seats on the Titanic." - Robert Scotellaro

57. Give Choices

Help avoid conflicts by giving your child a choice whenever possible, but limit those choices to two or three. For example, don't ask a young child, "What do you want for lunch?" The response might be, "Chocolate chip cookies!" Of course, you'll refuse, and then an argument might ensue. Instead ask, "Would you like a tuna sandwich, or grilled cheese?" This technique works well for older children, also. It helps them learn to make decisions, and to feel that their opinions are respected.

"The strongest principle of growth lies in human choice." - George Eliot

58. Quiet Time

One of the best things you can do for yourself and your children is to have "quiet time" each day. For children who are not yet in school and children who are home for the summer, set aside one or two hours at the same time every day. Each child goes to a separate room to nap, read or play with toys. If a toddler refuses to stay in his room, put a baby gate across the doorway and inform him that he must play quietly by himself for a while. Your children will probably resist this idea at first, but the benefits are worth the effort. One or two hours of complete peace and quiet each day will do wonders for everyone's stress level, and it will be reflected in the children's overall behavior.

"An inability to stay quiet is one of the most conspicuous failings of mankind." - Walter Bagehot

59. Pay Attention

Sometimes kids misbehave intentionally because it's the only way to get their parents' attention. In their minds, bad attention is better than no attention, and this applies to teenagers as well as toddlers. Take time each day to talk to your kids or play a game with them. Even if you've had a hard day at work, a few minutes of undivided attention is a worthwhile investment.

"You have to love your children unselfishly. That is hard. But it is the only way." - Barbara Bush

60. Bedtime Woes

For many parents, bedtime is the most dreaded time of the day. Endless requests for stories, glasses of water and one more hug can be exasperating. Instead, set some strict rules for bedtime and diligently enforce them: one story, one glass of water, and no leaving the room except to use the bathroom. If a toddler refuses to stay in her room, put a baby gate up in the doorway. Turn on a small nightlight to eliminate the excuse of being afraid of the dark, then leave the room and don't come back. The first few nights will be difficult, but if you stick with it, your bedtime woes are over.

"There never was a child so lovely but his mother was glad to get him asleep." - Ralph Waldo Emerson

61. What Time is Bedtime?

Unless your lifestyle or schedule deem otherwise, young children should be put to bed at least two hours before you and your spouse retire. Not only is this important for your own peace and well-being, but it's also important for your marriage. Time alone together is a rare commodity for most parents today, but it's easily attained by putting the kids to bed at an early hour, and insisting they stay there.

"Early to bed and early to rise makes a man healthy, wealthy and wise." John Clarke

62. Lights Out

If the kids aren't sleepy at their appointed bedtime, allow them to keep a reading light on for a half hour or an hour. Young children can be allowed to play quietly with their toys during this time, and older children can read. In fact, your child's reading skills may improve dramatically if he now finds himself with nothing else to do but read each evening.

"Reading not only enlarges and challenges the mind; it also engages and exercises the brain."
- Richard M. Nixon

63. Bedtime Is Not a Social Hour

If your home is large enough to give each child their own bedroom, this tip won't apply. For many people, however, having more than one child in a room at bedtime can result in non-stop chatter instead of quiet reading time. If this is a problem, just separate the kids. The oldest child can read in Mom & Dad's bedroom for a while, and return to her room after her sister has fallen asleep.

"First you have to teach a child to talk, then you have to teach it to be quiet." - Prochnow

64. Caring for Younger Siblings

Insist that your children help to take care of their younger siblings. Give them responsibilities according to their age and maturity. A child as young as three can fetch diapers and pacifiers. A seven-year-old can change a wet diaper and fill a bottle. A ten-year-old can supervise young children and prepare snacks.

"Provision for others is the fundamental responsibility of human life." - Woodrow Wilson

65. Taking Care of Themselves

Encourage your children to take care of their own needs whenever possible. By the age of four, a child can learn to play and rewind tapes in the VCR. By the age of five, a child can pour his own breakfast cereal. By insisting that your children take care of themselves as much as possible, they'll learn how to think for themselves, and they'll learn responsibility and problem solving skills as well.

"It is not what you do for your children, but what you have taught them to do for themselves that will make them successful human beings." - Ann Landers

66. Five-Minute Warning

No one likes to stop what they're doing without at least some warning, even children. Give a five-minute warning to your kids before calling them to dinner. Tell them they have five minutes to finish playing, and then they must stop and put away the toys. This helps to avoid conflicts before bedtime as well.

"Always be nice to your children because they are the ones who will choose your rest home." - Phyllis Diller

67. Immaturity or Willful Disobedience?

Expecting too much from a child can result in frustration for both child and parents. Take into consideration the child's age and capabilities, and never punish for something that might be caused by immaturity. For example, young children need to be reminded to pick up their toys and brush their teeth. If they still don't do it after being reminded, that's disobedience.

"There are three ways to get something done: do it yourself, employ someone, or forbid your children to do it." - Monta Crane

68. Traveling

E ven the most well-behaved kids find it difficult to be quiet and still during long trips. You can help them by purchasing a small assortment of diversions like crayons, pad of paper, playing cards, mini video games, books and mini puzzles. Surprise the children with these new items after the trip begins, but not before.

"There are two classes of travel - first class and with children." - Robert Benchley

69. Picky Eaters

Most children are picky eaters, and trying to force them to eat something they don't like is always a losing battle. Prepare nutritious foods for your child, and give him a simple choice: eat, or be hungry. Don't ever offer to make the child something different to eat. This just reinforces the negative behavior. He must eat what you've prepared for the family, or he doesn't eat at all. If the child chooses not to eat, then let him suffer the consequences and be hungry until the next meal is served.

"As a child, my family's menu consisted of two choices: Take it or leave it." - Buddy Hackett

70. Save it for Later

An additional way to deal with picky eaters is to save your child's uneaten meal, and when he complains of hunger before the next mealtime, serve it to him again. Once again, the choice is his, and if he still chooses not to eat, you shouldn't feel guilty about it because it was his own decision.

> *"My mother made me eat broccoli. I hate broccoli. I am the President of the United States. I will not eat any more broccoli." George Bush*

71. Nutritious Foods First

If a child is allowed to fill up on dinner rolls, she will have no incentive to eat the entree and vegetables. Instead, tell her she will not be allowed to have the bread until she has taken a few bites of her dinner. It might even be necessary to give the child one item at a time. For example, only after eating her salad will she be allowed to have the items she likes better.

> *"I will make an end of my dinner; there's pippins and cheese to come." - William Shakespeare*

72. Cleaning the Plate

Sometimes a child will eat nutritious foods, but very little of them. Mealtime stress occurs when parents try to force children to eat everything on their plates. Not only does this cause unnecessary strife, but it can also lead to eating disorders and adult obesity. A child's appetite varies considerably from day to day, and is greatly affected by growth stages. Avoid conflict by putting only a small amount of each item on your child's plate, allowing her to have a second serving if she desires it.

"We never repent of having eaten too little."
- Thomas Jefferson

73. Limit the Sugar

Some studies have shown that sugar does not affect the behavior of children, but many parents disagree. These parents have witnessed sugar's ill effects on their children, and they are convinced it causes hyperactivity. Observe your children before and after eating sweet foods and perhaps you'll see a correlation. Be aware, also, that many foods contain sugar, even the ones you wouldn't expect: crackers, peanut butter, yogurt, flavored potato chips, etc. Read the ingredients on your favorite brands to discover how much sugar your child is actually consuming each day. It may be the cause of his misbehavior.

"Even when freshly washed and relieved of all obvious confections, children tend to be sticky."
- Fran Lebowitz

74. Food Allergies

Some children behave poorly because of chemicals in their diet. Allergies to food additives such as artificial coloring and preservatives can cause children to misbehave, even though they are trying their best not to. By keeping track of what your child consumes, you might notice some correlation between his diet and his behavior. Eliminate the suspect foods, and see if the behavior improves.

"In general, my children refuse to eat anything that hasn't danced on TV." - Erma Bombeck

75. Disruptive Behavior in a Group

Schools deal with this problem by temporarily banishing the child. It works well at parties and other social gatherings as well. If a child is being disruptive, have him sit somewhere else, separated from the others. His desire to participate will overcome his desire to be disruptive.

"Everyone is in awe of the lion tamer in a cage with half a dozen lions - everyone but a school bus driver."
- Anonymous

76. Discipline in Public

It's easy to tell which parents are afraid to discipline in public. They're the ones who say, "I don't understand it. She never acts this way at home!" Apparently, those children know that they can get away with misbehavior because their parents will not enforce behavioral rules while away from home. It's important to discipline your children for misbehavior no matter where you are. If you're visiting at a friend's home, excuse yourself for a moment, and then take your child aside to deal with the inappropriate behavior. If you don't deal with the misbehavior quickly and efficiently, the child will be tempted to break rules just because she knows she can get away with it.

"A child left to himself disgraces his mother."
- Proverbs 29:15

77. Keep Them Fed and Rested

When kids are hungry or tired, even the best of them will misbehave. You can avoid many problems if you make sure that your children get at least eight hours of sleep each night, and always keep snacks handy for those times when meals are delayed.

"Principles have no real force except when one is well fed." - Mark Twain

OLDER
CHILDREN

78. Sibling Rivalry

When children are constantly bickering and fighting with each other, everyone in the house is affected. Some parents accept this type of behavior as being natural and unavoidable. Parents of peaceful, well-behaved children know differently. It's best to establish a no-tolerance policy for sibling fights and then strictly enforce it. For pre-teens, when an argument breaks out, immediately warn the children that they will be separated if they continue. If they do continue, follow through with your threat and immediately send them to separate rooms for 10 or 15 minutes of seclusion. For older kids, revoke privileges. Repeat this as often as necessary until the children learn to settle their differences peacefully.

"How good and pleasant it is when brothers dwell in unity." - Psalms 133:1

79. Balance and Moderation

By teaching your child the concepts of balance and moderation, you will benefit him in many ways. For example, you can enrich a child's mind and help to improve his grades by balancing TV with reading. (One hour of television is allowed after a certain number of pages are read.) You can help a child to learn moderation with methods such as allowing candy only one day a week, perhaps on Sunday. When offered candy on other days, your child must either reject it, or save it for Sunday. By doing this, you can help him learn to just say "No." (It's valuable practice for resisting peer pressure.) As additional benefits, your child will learn about the rewards of delayed gratification, and he'll have healthier teeth, too!

"It's all about balance, and balance is a valuable lesson to learn for those times when you're not around."
- Victoria Sutherland

80. Being Considerate of Others

Teach your child to be considerate of others by modeling this behavior yourself. Hold doors open for people, and encourage your children to do so as well. Give up your seats on the bus to elderly people and pregnant women. Help your neighbor carry in her groceries, and have the children bring her soup when she's ill. Demonstrate unselfish behavior for your children as often as possible, and encourage them to follow your lead.

"Children have never been very good at listening to their elders, but they have never failed to imitate them." - James Baldwin

81. The Oldest Child

Every member of the family should contribute to the household duties, but all too often, the oldest child ends up with an unfair share. When this happens, the child could become resentful towards her parents and her younger siblings. Remember to be fair. If you would like your teenager to babysit her younger siblings, once-a-week free babysitting is not too much to ask. If you require her services more than once a week, pay her for her time. In this way, you'll be showing respect for her, as well as giving her a chance to earn money.

"A babysitter is a teenage girl you hire to let your children do whatever they want." - Henny Youngman

82. Discipline Privately

Rules must always be enforced, but you should never reprimand your child in front of her friends. Embarrassment and humiliation can damage a child's self-esteem, and often leads to resentment and rebellion. If your child is misbehaving while friends are present, politely ask her to join you in another room, and discuss the problem there.

"Speak well of your friend in public, admonish in secret." - Publius Syrus

83. Don't Nag

Constant nagging and strife only cause stress for both parent and child. When a child discovers that there is no threat behind all the millions of words thrown at him, he stops listening to them. Not only is nagging ineffective, but it's also counter productive. Children lose respect for parents who nag, and the parents become increasingly unnerved and frustrated. It's better to just administer proper discipline swiftly and judiciously.

"Respect the child. Be not too much his parent. Trespass not on his solitude." - Ralph Waldo Emerson

84. Suffering the Consequences

Don't be quick to bail your child out when he gets himself into trouble. If a child is not allowed to experience the consequences of his mistakes, he will make those same mistakes again. For example, if your son breaks a neighbor's window with a baseball, he should pay for it with his own allowance. Even though it was an accident, he will have learned a valuable lesson from the experience, and will always remember the high price of carelessness.

"At every step the child should be allowed to meet the real experiences of life; the thorns should never be plucked from his roses." - Ellen Key

85. Allowances Should be Earned

One of the best ways to instill a work ethic in your children and prepare them for the real world is to insist that they "earn" their allowance. Adults must work for their money, so why not children? Decide on a suitable amount, taking into consideration the child's age and the family's financial status. Then withhold some or all of that amount if the child has not faithfully completed his chores that week.

"Hard work spotlights the character of people: some turn up their sleeves, some turn up their noses, and some don't turn up at all." - Sam Ewing

86. Taking a Stand

Don't take a stand on an issue until you are sure you've made the right decision. If you tell your teenager that she can't go to a party and then change your mind later, your child has learned that "No" doesn't really mean "No." If she responded to the initial decision in typical teenager fashion (slamming doors, arguing, sulking), then she'll believe these techniques worked, and she'll employ them every time.

"Think before you speak." - George Washington

87. Laziness

It's common for an adolescent's body to go through periods of tremendous growth, and these growth periods may cause him or her to have a greater need for sleep. Many parents are annoyed by this apparent "laziness," but they shouldn't be overly concerned; it will eventually pass. In the meantime, try offering incentives to get your teenager off the couch and into an activity.

"Laziness: the habit of resting before fatigue sets in."
- Jules Renard

88. Discuss Improvement

After a child has been disciplined, have a short discussion about what happened. Give her suggestions as to how she could have handled the situation differently. This works best if you wait until things are calm and emotions have subsided.

89. Constant Requests

If you only buy toys and other items for your children at birthdays and Christmas, they won't beg you constantly to buy things for them. If they ask for something at any other time of the year, tell them to save their allowance for it, or else put it on their Christmas list and wait.

"A truly appreciative child will break, lose, spoil, or fondle to death any really successful gift within a matter of minutes." - Russell Lynes

90. Television Influence

Children's television has changed dramatically in the last few years. A typical cartoon no longer consists of a cat trying to catch a canary. Children's programming today is much more sophisticated. Many of the cartoons glorify disrespect, violence and rejection of authority, all for the amusement of their young audiences. Repeated exposure to these attitudes can rub off on kids and affect their behavior.

"All television is educational television. The only question is, what is it teaching?"
- Nicholas Johnson, FCC chairman

91. Internet Influence

A parent should never allow unsupervised access to the Internet. Children can be easily led astray by the information they find on-line. Most parents are aware of the availability of hardcore pornography, but that's not the only danger. Some "chat" rooms and message boards are unregulated areas where children and teens can befriend each other and carry on conversations which their parents wouldn't approve of. Topics regularly include promoting and glorifying sex, drugs, violence, rebellion, prejudice and hate. The best way to protect your child from this is to allow Internet usage only in a room where an adult will be present at all times.

> *"Monitor your child's use of on-line services, just as you would any of his entertainment activities."*
> *- Jan Wagner, SAFE-T-CHILD founder*

92. Put Them to Work

Here's a technique for dealing with older kids: When they're good, leave them alone. When they start bickering with each other or otherwise getting on your nerves, put them to work. (Pulling weeds, washing the car, cleaning the garage, etc.) The children will quickly learn that it pays to be good!

"Work keeps at bay three great evils: boredom, vice, and need." - Voltaire

93. Fashion Battles

Children can be very obstinate when it comes to what clothes and shoes they'll wear. Most will insist on wearing the latest fashions, regardless of how unflattering and/or expensive they are. A good way to deal with this is to compromise. Make it clear to your child that if you are paying for the clothes, you will buy only the items you approve of. If the child wants something expensive or unattractive, he may have it, but he must pay for it with his own money.

"I have seen my children struggle into the kitchen in the morning with outfits that need only one accessory: an empty gin bottle." - Erma Bombeck

94. Bad Attitudes

A child with a bad attitude can make life miserable for everyone in the home. For infrequent occurrences, send the child to her room, and tell her she is not to come out until her attitude has improved. For chronic attitude problems, set up an incentive program to encourage her to change. Choose a reward which appeals greatly to her, then tell her she can earn that reward only by maintaining a pleasant attitude for 30 days. An attitude is like a habit, and by the time she reaches the goal, the positive change may be permanent.

"Bad habits are easier to abandon today than tomorrow." - Yiddish saying

95. Don't Overindulge Them

Children who are given everything they want tend to appreciate nothing and be very demanding. Even if you can afford to give your children everything, you shouldn't. You'll be depriving them of the joy that comes from working hard towards a goal and achieving it. People who are overindulged as children frequently grow up to be adults who don't have a strong work ethic and are thus ill-equipped to function in society.

"Do not handicap your children by making their lives easy." - Lazarus Long

96. Mutual Benefits

An easy way to get children to do things for you is by learning to say "Yes" conditionally. For example, when your child asks to spend the night at a friend's house, say, "Yes, if you mow the lawn first." If your child asks for money, say, "Yes, if you clean the garage first." This way, the children have their requests granted, and you'll receive something in return.

"The word 'no' carries a lot more meaning when spoken by a parent who also knows how to say 'yes'."
- Joyce Maynard

97. Express Gratitude

When your children are being especially helpful or considerate, write little thank-you notes complimenting them on their actions, and leave them around the house where they will be found. Your children will be more likely to continue this good behavior when they know their efforts are appreciated.

"How often we can meet someone to whom we owe a debt of gratitude without thinking about it at all."
- Goethe

98. Clean Their Rooms

For some reason, most children have an aversion to straightening up their rooms. You can make the job easier for them by insisting they get rid of unnecessary clutter, then give away or throw away anything they don't use. If your child doesn't do a good job of cleaning his room after he's been told to, try this: Take everything you find in his room which hasn't been put away properly, and put it into a box. Then hide that box in your closet for two weeks. After being deprived of the use of his favorite toys and clothes for a while, your child will be more inclined to clean his room properly.

"A place for everything and everything in its place."
- Isabella Mary Beeton

99. No Arguments

It's frustrating to have a child ask for something again and again after being told, "No." Establish a policy of zero tolerance on this. Make it clear that repeated requests and arguing with a parent is strictly not allowed and will result in punishment every time.

"There is nothing wrong with teenagers that reasoning with them won't aggravate." - Anonymous

100. Don t Expect Perfection

Children are not small adults. They don't have the wisdom and self-control which comes with maturity, and even the most well-behaved children will have bad moments. When a parent expects too much, children may feel that they can't possibly live up to the parent's expectations and will cease trying. To avoid this, always be fair and consistent, and above all else, love unconditionally!

"Stop trying to perfect your child, but keep trying to perfect your relationship with him." - Dr. Henker

Order Information

To obtain extra copies of *Well-Behaved Children: 100 Tips From Parents Who Have Them,* send $9.95 plus $2.50 for shipping and handling for the first book ($1.00 shipping and handling for each additional book) to:

BookMasters, Inc.
P.O. Box 388
Ashland, OH 44805

Number of books requested: _____

Total Enclosed: _____

Ship to: _____

_____

_____

Telephone orders: (800) 247-6553
Fax orders: (419) 281-6883
E-mail orders: order@bookmasters.com
Visa, MasterCard, Discover, and American Express accepted.

Quantity discounts available upon request.

Order Information

To obtain extra copies of *Well-Behaved Children: 100 Tips From Parents Who Have Them*, send $9.95 plus $2.50 for shipping and handling for the first book ($1.00 shipping and handling for each additional book) to:

BookMasters, Inc.
P.O. Box 388
Ashland, OH 44805

Number of books requested: _____

Total Enclosed: _____

Ship to: _____

_____

_____

Telephone orders: (800) 247-6553
Fax orders: (419) 281-6883
E-mail orders: order@bookmasters.com
Visa, MasterCard, Discover, and American Express accepted.

Quantity discounts available upon request.